W9-BXF-045

ask *ali*

All the Advice You'll Ever Need

Edited by Ellen Pill Blooming, Ph.D.

Discovery Girls, Inc.

CALIFORNIA

Discovery Girls, Inc.
445 South San Antonio Rd, Ste. 205
Los Altos, California 94022

Ask Ali: All the Advice You'll Ever Need
Copyright © 2012 Discovery Girls, Inc.
Previously published as *The Fab Girls' Guide to Getting Your Questions Answered.*

Ask Ali illustrations by Aruna Rangarajan.

All DG Polls are from 2012 DiscoveryGirls.com.

ISBN 978-1-934766-10-1

Visit Discovery Girls' web site at www.discoverygirls.com.

Printed in the United States of America.

Dedication

Dedicated to the thousands of girls who have taken the time to write to *Discovery Girls* magazine to share your ideas, thoughts, personal stories, and yes, even your problems. All of us who work at Discovery Girls, Inc. have been deeply touched by your letters. You are a constant source of insight and inspiration, and the reason we have created this book.

Acknowledgments

I'd like to send a special thank you to all the girls who have read *Discovery Girls* magazine over the years and have generously shared your thoughts, ideas, and experiences with us. Without you, there would be no *Discovery Girls* magazine and definitely no Discovery Girls books. I feel so very lucky to have had the opportunity to work with my dedicated and talented staff: Julia Clause, Ashley DeGree, Naomi Kirsten, Katherine Inouye Lau, Alex Saymo, Bill Tsukuda, Sarah Verney, and interns Lyn Meheʻula, Laura Riparbelli, and Nick Tran. Your enthusiasm and ability to keep your sense of humor while meeting insane deadlines, your willingness to work long hours, your amazing creative energy, and your insistence on always striving to get better and better have meant more to me than you will ever know—my deepest appreciation!

Catherine Lee
PUBLISHER
DISCOVERY GIRLS, INC.

Contents

Introduction

When Did Life Get So Complicated?

You're the only girl in your class who has started to develop...so how do you deal with the stares and snickering when it's time to change for gym? You used to have six close friends, but they all dumped you for the popular crowd...and **now you have no one.** You're fine with being "just friends" with guys...so what do you do when your **boy-crazy friends pressure you** to have a *boyfriend*? And then there's the tougher stuff, like **coping with the death of a parent**, being asked to choose between your mom and dad in a divorce, and worrying about a best friend who may be getting hurt by a parent at home...

Whether you're at school, at home, or just hanging with your buds, **problems seem to find you everywhere.** No wonder you feel lost sometimes!

It's time to take back your life, girls! Discovery Girls' *Ask Ali: All the Advice You'll Ever Need* **is your must-have book** for dealing with life's most pressing problems. At *Discovery Girls* magazine,

we receive thousands of letters for Ali, our advice columnist—many more than we can possibly answer in the magazine. So, here, for the first time, Ali answers more of your questions than ever and tackles your toughest issues.

So press "pause" on the drama that is your life, settle in, and find out how to **deal with your problems** of yesterday, today, and tomorrow—starting now!

–The Editors of *Discovery Girls*

Chapter One

FRIENDSHIP

YOUR BFF DRAMAS MOST OFTEN REVOLVE AROUND:

- One friend wants to be more popular.
- Jealousy over having other friends.
- Silly fights that get out of control.

DG POLL!

Do you think your friends know the "real you"?

No! It feels like we're from different planets.	5%
I'm not sure who the "real me" is these days.	15%
I think they try but they don't understand what I'm going through.	30%
Definitely! They totally "get" me and we can talk about everything.	50%

Unpredictable Friend

Dear Ali,

I have this friend who is so fun when she's happy, but when she's not, she's the worst person in the world to be around. Half of the time we're best buds, and the other half we're making up rumors about the other and really hurting each other's feelings. It's really hard to stay away from her when she's happy. She's so full of life, which draws people to her. But then she turns on you and becomes the meanest, most selfish girl in school. Another thing is that when I am her friend, I want to tell her everything, even my deepest, darkest secrets. But when she's my enemy, she blabs everything I've told her. What do I do?

–Two-Faced Friends

Dear Two-Faced Friends,

You really have an unpredictable situation here! You can't change your friend's behavior, but you do have control over your own choices. What you have to do is to take responsibility for your own behavior—don't mimic her by becoming mean just because she does. You need to stay your friendly, nice, and trustworthy self, no matter what she does. Stay away when she's in one of her bad moods, and resolve to not tell her any of your secrets. Only tell her things that you wouldn't mind everyone knowing about, since you never know when or what she will blab. If you can live with these rules, you'll be okay. If not, you might just need to move away from this oh-so-dramatic friendship entirely.

We're best buds—and sworn enemies!

Not Happy for Me

Dear Ali,

Ever since I got a part in the school play and my friend didn't, she's been acting weird. I have been leaving class to practice, and when I get back she gives me this mean glare. At lunch, I sit down next to her and I try to talk to her, but she quickly changes the subject and then walks off. My friends tell me that she is talking about me behind my back. I don't want to lose a good friend. What do I do?

—Losing My Friend

Dear Losing My Friend,

It sounds like your friend has a bad case of jealousy. You've done nothing wrong, but she's having a hard time dealing with not getting the part in the play. Try to be sensitive about how difficult this is for her. How would you feel if she'd gotten in and you hadn't? Let her know that you don't want this to affect your friendship. You might say something like, "Next time you'll probably get a part and I won't!" And are there are opportunities for her to help with the play? There are important backstage jobs, and they're sometimes even more fun than acting! If you can talk it through, you may be able to help her deal with her jealousy.

ali

Trying Too Hard

Dear Ali,

My friend Kyla is a great friend, but not a lot of people think so. By "a lot," I mean the rest of my friends! I know that Kyla is trying too hard to be popular. She tries to be funny, but she's not. But when you get to know her like I have, you like her the way she is. How can I get her to just relax and show her true self?

-Friend 911

Dear Friend 911,

You are a true friend for taking the time to get to know Kyla and for sticking by her. Keep in mind that you can't make her act differently, but you can let her know what you think. Tell her that she is a terrific person and a good friend, but when she tries too hard to be something she's not, people can't see how wonderful she really is. Suggest that she stop trying so hard to be liked and see what happens. The rest is up to her!

ali

Need Friends Now!

Dear Ali,

I don't have friends! It isn't fair. When there's a project at school, nobody wants to work on it with me. I used to have six friends but they all dumped me to become popular. I want a friend that I can talk to when I'm upset or else I'll go nuts! Should I have a party so girls could notice that I'm a great friend? Please! Please! Give me advice on finding friends!

—Friendless

Dear Friendless,

Sometimes it's hard to pinpoint what went wrong in a friendship. Maybe you can ask one of the girls why you're not being included anymore. Then, do your best to listen without getting defensive. You might learn something that's useful for future friendships. As far as making new friends, a party usually isn't a good solution. If they ignore you at school, they'll probably ignore you at a party. Instead try to be a good friend, one-on-one. Stop waiting to be picked for class projects. Try talking to someone new at lunch. Invite a girl to work on homework together after school. Ask someone to the movies. When your old friends see you laughing with new friends, they might want to join the fun!

ali

Can't Trust Her

Dear Ali,

Every time I call one of my friends to do stuff, she makes up excuses about why she can't come, but I know that she's really hanging out with her other friends. When I'm with her, she says she doesn't like the other girls, but I think she probably says the same thing about me to them! I can't ask the other girls in her group, because we don't like each other! What should I do?

—Confused

Dear Confused,

This isn't easy, but friendships always take a bit of hard work to grow strong. You need to ask this girl what's going on. She may feel she can't be up front with you about her friendship with the other girls because you'll want her to choose between you and them. Or she may just be trying to spare your feelings. On the other hand, your talk might confirm your feeling that she's only acting like a friend to your face while bad-mouthing you behind your back. If that's the case, you'll probably want to concentrate on your other friends. Either way, it's always worth it to try talking things through!

ali

Bad Influence?

Dear Ali,

One of my friends has a really bad cussing problem. I hear her cussing so much that I've started to cuss too. Everyone says I've changed since I started hanging around her, and I feel like I have. She makes fun of people and uses cuss words to describe other students as well as the teacher. I don't like to do any of that. Now her family is in the process of choosing middle schools and she might go to mine. I just have so many mixed feelings! Please help me! What should I do?

—Sick of Swearing

Dear Sick of Swearing,

I read your letter twice to see if you said anything good about this friend, and guess what? You didn't. I'm sure she has some good qualities, but sometimes you have to decide if the friendship is worth the price. Using cuss words is a bad habit that can get you in hot water in a lot of situations. You have no control over whether or not she ends up in your school, but you can control whether or not you spend time with her. If the friendship is really important to you, you can tell her the cussing and being mean really bothers you. Give her a chance to change. But if she can't (or won't), maybe it's time to find some new friends.

ali

Stop the Copying!

Dear Ali,

My best friend is funny and is there when I need someone to talk to. But she also copies me. I dance competitively and she tries to do the moves but she does them wrong. Everybody always cheers for her—when I'm the one who taught her how to do them! I know I'm supposed to take her copying as a compliment, but it's hard. I also know she thinks I'm pretty, smart, and talented, because she wrote me a letter about it. She needs to find the good things about herself instead of copying me. It shouldn't take her too long, because I found them in the first five minutes after I met her.

—Copycatee

Dear Copycatee,

You've solved your own problem and you don't even know it! The last thing you said in your letter is a beautiful tribute to your friend and to how much she means to you. You need to tell her how you feel. It might not be easy, but it's the only way to clear the air. Tell her what an amazing friend she is. Then tell her that it bothers you that she sometimes tries to copy the things you do. Let her know that it hurts your feelings when she puts you down. And, most important, tell her that you wish she'd see the amazing girl she is—and that she doesn't need to copy anyone!

ali

My best friend read my diary!

Friend or Frenemy?

Dear Ali,

I need help! I invited my BFF for a sleepover and she found my diary and read it. It had things in it about boys I like. The next morning, she told me what she had done and promised that she could keep a secret. I trusted her but she told everyone at school. Now kids keep teasing me. I told her that if she didn't stop, we couldn't be friends anymore, but she didn't care. I lost all my friends so I started hanging out with the boys. And then she told everyone that I like them. Now they won't be my friends either. Why would a BFF I thought I could trust go behind my back? Please help me.

—Betrayed

Dear Betrayed,

A real friend would never do what this girl did. The best thing you can do now is to ignore her comments. When she starts spreading rumors or sharing your secrets, just say something like, "I'm flattered that everyone's so interested in my life, but most of what she says isn't true, and it sure isn't that interesting!" If someone says they won't be your friend because of what this girl is telling them, try saying something like, "I think it's sad that you would give up being my friend because of her gossip." Dealing with comments in a brief and matter-of-fact way is your best bet. With some time, your ex-BFF will fade out of the spotlight and you'll have some great new friends!

Feuding BFFs

Dear Ali,

I have two best friends and usually we all get along great, but last week they got in a big fight. Every day they both tell me why they are right and beg me to take their side. I keep telling them I don't want to, but they don't stop! I'm really tired of hearing about this stupid fight and I just want them to be friends again. What should I do?

—Caught in the Middle

Dear Caught in the Middle,

It's so unfair of your friends to put you in this position—good for you for sticking to what you know is right! Your best bet is to take each of them aside and tell her that, as much as you value her friendship, you can't take sides because you value the other girl's friendship, too. You could add that you really just wish the three of you could get back to being friends again and ask if there's anything you can do (*besides* taking sides!) to help them make up. Hopefully they'll find a way to work it out, but if they can't, you can still continue to be friends with each of them separately.

New and Not Happy

Dear Ali,

I used to live in Missouri, but I recently moved to California. I really hate it here, and I'm not making a very good impression in my class. Two girls in particular are being mean to me. This grade has been together since kindergarten, and they don't want me to make friends. How can I break into a small group and learn to like California more?

—Miserable in Malibu

Dear Miserable in Malibu,

It's always hard to be new in a school when all the other kids have known each other for a long time! You probably won't be accepted by everyone all at once, but making just one friend can make a world of difference. Is there someone in the group that has been a little friendlier than the others? Ask her over after school, maybe to do homework together. You'll probably find it a lot easier to make friends when you're only dealing with one person, not a group. And remember to stay upbeat! If your new classmates get the impression you liked everything better "back home," they might feel like you really don't like them (even if it's not true!).

ali

Need to Breathe!

Dear Ali,

I have a really good friend whom I have known since third grade. Lately she has been crowding me and keeping me from being with my other friends at school. My other friends have also noticed. I really want to talk to her about it, but I don't know how. I don't want our friendship to end because of this.

—Crowded

Dear Crowded,

The only way for your friend to know you're having a problem with her is for you to talk about it. It isn't always easy, but here are some guidelines:

- Find a place that is private, where you won't be overheard or interrupted.
- Make sure you aren't angry—you want to have a nice, polite discussion.
- Talk about how you feel. Use "I" statements, like, "I feel bad that I can't hang out with my other friends without hurting your feelings."

She may not even realize how her behavior is affecting you. Give her a chance to change, and be patient. If she can't get over her clinginess, though, you may want to hang out with other friends for a while.

Ali

☆ ☆ ☆

My Fault!

Dear Ali,

I told my friend some lies when I said I wouldn't hurt her feelings. Then she figured out that I was lying to her and now she won't talk to me. What can I do to make her talk to me again?

—Liar

✫ ✫ ✫

Dear Liar,

You can't "make" someone talk to you or forgive you. You can only give your very best effort to do what you know is right and see what happens. It's hard to know what exactly happened with you and your friend. If you were trying to protect her feelings by lying, you need to explain that to her. If it was a different circumstance, you need to explain why you felt the need to lie. If she won't listen to you, try explaining yourself in a letter. Let her know why you did it, apologize, and remind her how important her friendship is to you.

Money Matters

Dear Ali,

My friend is <u>always</u> borrowing my money! She is always short a dollar or two and says, "I swear I'll pay you back." The problem is that she never does. It's so hard to bring it up and she can't take a hint. Please help me!

—Broke

Dear Broke,

Your friend is a freeloader! And right now she doesn't have any reason to change because the situation is working for her. *Why* is it working? Because you keep loaning her money! I know you want to be nice and trust her, but you're just perpetuating the problem. Don't just cut her off, though. Let her know what she owes you and that you'll be glad to give her a loan again *after* she's paid you back. Don't sound angry, hurt, or annoyed, just matter-of-fact, and make sure the conversation is private—just the two of you. Spell it out clearly up front, and you won't have to agonize over it every time—just be sure to stick to your rules!

ali

My friend is always borrowing money...

Can't Take It

Dear Ali,

I have this friend and she is being really mean to me. She always leaves me out of things in school and it is very upsetting. And I have no parents so it is really, really hard for me. I have to cope with people teasing me because I'm an orphan. I wish they would stop. What should I do?

—All Alone

Dear All Alone,

It can be hard to accept, but if a friend isn't being nice and keeps leaving you out, she has probably moved on. I know it must be especially hard for you to lose a friend since you don't have parents. If you can talk to your caregiver or to another adult you trust, please share your concerns with them and see if they can help you find ways to fit in. Find kids who *don't* tease, and start to make some new friends. Be open and sincere without being pushy, and you'll find new friends who will include you and be nice. It might take some time, but soon you'll start to feel like you've got some friends who believe in you.

ali

Everything Changed!

Dear Ali,

I once had two best friends, Stephanie and Kim, and then Stephanie moved away. I thought it would be okay—that I could still talk to Stephanie on the phone and still have Kim over. But once Stephanie moved away, Kim started hanging out with this other girl and is ignoring me. I've invited her over but she just isn't the same. She didn't gradually ignore me, either—she just dropped me like a hot potato. I don't understand why because I haven't done anything to upset her. I want to be her best friend again, but how?

-Left Behind

Dear Left Behind,

It can be tough when friends move, and it sounds like Kim has tried to adjust to Stephanie's absence in her own way. Maybe when she's with you, she misses Stephanie since you three used to hang out together. To find out what's going on for sure, you need to talk with Kim. Let her know that you miss spending time with her and you miss your friendship. Then just ask her, honestly and sincerely, why she's been ignoring you. Hopefully, she'll give you some answers and be open to working on your friendship. If not, at least you'll know what's really going on and you can start finding some new friends. And, of course, you can still talk and write to Stephanie!

Chapter Two

FAMILY

YOUR TOP 3 FAMILY FEARS ARE:

- Your parents getting a divorce.
- Losing a family member.
- Your parents not understanding you.

DG POLL!

My biggest family pet peeve is...

Sharing the bathroom. I never get in there first!	8%
Not getting enough freedom!	27%
Putting up with nosy little brothers or sisters.	28%
Arguing. Why can't we all just get along?	37%

My mom won't let me buy it!

My Money, My Clothes

Dear Ali,

Every time my mom and I go shopping for clothes, I see something that I really like that she won't let me have. It could be the saying on the shirt or the pattern on some Capris. I even offer to pay for it myself, but if she doesn't like it, I can't get it. I'm the one wearing the clothes! How come if my mom doesn't like it, I can't get it, even if I pay for it?

—Fashion Foiled

Dear Fashion Foiled,

Wow—what a frustrating situation! If your mom is rejecting your choices because she thinks they're not appropriate for someone your age, you may have to live by her rules for now. But if you simply have different tastes, you may be able to talk her into a compromise—if you handle the situation maturely. Pick a time when she's not rushed or stressed and tell her that you've been thinking a lot about this and want to understand her point of view, and that you hope she'll listen to yours. Listen carefully to what her objections are and try to calmly address them, one by one. Hopefully she'll see that you're growing up and deserve the chance to make some of your own clothing choices.

Too Busy

Dear Ali,

I have so many activities all the time! I never get to just do nothing or hang out with my friends. My mom always wants me to try everything. I like some of the sports I do but don't really want to do piano, ballet, and swimming too. But she won't let me quit <u>anything</u>. She just says I'm so lucky to have so many opportunities and I should do my best at everything. Help me, please!

—Overloaded

Dear Overloaded,

Maybe your mom didn't have all these opportunities when she was a girl, and she wants to be sure that you do? That's wonderful, but she needs to understand how overloaded you feel. Tell her you love her and that you appreciate that she's giving you these opportunities. Next, explain to her that when you have so many activities, you can't possibly do your best at all of them. Ask her if you can continue with just two activities for the next few months, and take a break from the others. Suggest she choose one of the activities and you choose the other, and promise to work especially hard at them. Then make sure you hold up your end of the bargain!

ali

Dear Ali,

I need some advice. My younger sister uses web sites that are too old for her. She's been keeping it a secret and I've seen her on them more than once. Is there any way that I can get her to stop without her hating me?

—Web-Surfing Sister

Dear Web-Surfing Sister,

Have you tried talking to her? Nicely let her know that you have noticed that she's on some inappropriate sites and you're worried. If you share a computer, you might tell her that you're afraid that you might get in trouble if your parents check the web sites visited. You might also ask your parents to put parental controls on the computer because when you do a search online, sometimes web sites come up that aren't appropriate for you and you don't want to have to worry about that. If that won't work, you'll have to tell your parents. Your sister may be mad for a while, but isn't it worth enduring her anger to keep her safe?

ali

Problems at Home

Dear Ali,

My parents fight a lot and my dad drinks a lot. My dad will say some little thing and then my mom goes ballistic about it. I'm scared they will get a divorce. I really love both my mom and dad. I don't want anything to jeopardize their relationship. I think I make things worse for them. It must be my fault. Help me, please!

—My Fault

Dear My Fault,

Listen very carefully: *It's not your fault.* As much as you want your parents to stay together, you have no control over their relationship. The best thing you can do is to talk to your parents separately and tell them how upset you get when they fight. If you let them know that you are worried that they might divorce, they may be able to help you understand the situation better. *They're* responsible for what happens between them, and if they do divorce, they'll do the best they can to take care of you. All you can do is to love your parents and try to respect their decisions, whatever they are.

Clowning Around?

Dear Ali,

My parents make jokes about me and tease me and they think it's funny. They don't know that their jokes really hurt my feelings. I tried telling them how I feel, but they just tell me they're kidding around. Most of the jokes make me feel worthless and some of them just hurt inside. I feel I can't go to my parents for advice anymore. Please help me!

—No Joke

Dear No Joke,

No doubt your parents really are just teasing. They don't mean any harm by what they're saying, so it's hard for them to understand how you feel. Since things are unlikely to change unless they do understand, you'll have to try again to get your point across. Be sure to tell them that you know they are not trying to hurt you, but it's gotten so bad that you feel you can't talk to them anymore, and that makes you really sad. If they *still* don't get it, talk to another adult you trust—a teacher, aunt, cousin, grandparent, or school counselor—who may be able to help your parents understand. Don't give up...you are *not* worthless, and you don't deserve all this hurt.

ali

Unclean Scene

Dear Ali,

My house is such a disgusting mess all the time. My family is really messy. I'm totally embarrassed to have my friends over. I'm afraid they will tell everyone at my school. They already think something is wrong at my house because I haven't had anyone over yet. What can I do?

—Not a Neat Freak

Dear Not a Neat Freak,

Wow, that's a tough situation to be in. Try having a serious talk with your family to let them know how important this is to you. Make sure you handle the situation with some tact, though! *Don't* accuse them of being slobs. Instead, tell them you're uncomfortable having people over when the house is messy, and suggest a family clean-up day. If they know this means a lot to you *and* you volunteer to do some of the work, you should get the results you want. If not, you'll simply have to take matters into your own hands and clean, clean, clean! Good luck!

Dear Ali,

My mom and I fight all the time. Sometimes we fight over stupid things, like whether I did my chores or not. Other times, it's about nothing at all. I have gone to several people but none of them have helped. My mom thinks we fight because my parents recently divorced, but that's not it. I don't know what it is or what to do. Please help me!

—Mad at Mom

Dear Mad at Mom,

It's common for girls to fight more with their moms as they get closer to their teen years. As you become more independent it's almost inevitable that you'll clash from time to time. It's also possible that your mom is right when she says you're fighting because of your parents' divorce. Even though it doesn't *feel* like that's the problem, you could be angry at her, at your dad, or just at the universe for putting you through all that upset. It might help to tell your mom you want to get along better. Listen to her point of view and tell her you hope she'll try to listen to yours. Hopefully she'll meet you halfway. Hang in there—it will get better with time.

ali

Oh, Brother!

Dear Ali,

My problem is my twin brother. My mom thinks we should appreciate each other, but I really don't like him. When I wear nice clothes and make cool things, he says I look ugly or "That's ugly." He steals my stuff, including my library card. He thinks I am a show-off but I don't think I am. Why can't we be friends? Help!

—Unhappy Twin

Dear Unhappy Twin,

Brothers and sisters often fight while they are growing up, only to become friends as adults. Perhaps you and your brother are having a difficult time because, as twins, everyone expects you to be super close. There are some things you can do to try to get along better, but *do* keep one thing in mind: You can't change the way your brother behaves. You can only change how *you* act. Try a little experiment: Treat him nicely for a week. Refuse to fight with him or insult him. Ignore his teasing. You may be surprised to find that if *you* change, he will, too. It's unlikely that you'll stop fighting for good, but there's a good chance you can improve things considerably.

ali

My brother and I don't get along!

Not a Baby!

Dear Ali,

I can't get along with my parents. I'm almost 13 and they won't even let me walk to a park by myself. (The park is less than a block away!) They are too overprotective. My friends say things like, "You'll be thankful later!" but I feel like they're strangling me! I have been wishing they were different since I was seven. How can I make them trust me?

—Overprotected

Dear Overprotected,

Have you asked your parents why they're so protective? If it's not because of something you've done and you've never given them reason to distrust your judgment, your best bet is to calmly ask them for a little slack. Suggest some *small* changes to start, and then make sure you stick to any conditions they set forth. For example, maybe they'll agree to let you walk to the park with a friend, or if you call them when you get there. If they still won't give an inch, try asking another adult you trust—an aunt, grandparent, or teacher—to help convince them that you're old enough to have a bit more freedom.

ali

Dear Ali,

I've got a big problem. I live with my mom and step-dad. My real dad lives in Mexico, but my stepdad hates it when my real dad calls me. Sometimes I cry and get mad at my stepdad. I don't get why he doesn't let me talk to my real dad. Ali, please help me.

—Missing Dad

Dear Missing Dad,

It's hard being separated from a parent, and not being allowed to speak with your dad must make it even worse. What if you reminded your mom that you love her and your stepdad, but that you also love your real dad? It's possible your stepdad is acting out of concern for you. He may think your dad is not a responsible father and is trying to protect you by keeping you from having too much contact with him. On the other hand, he may just be jealous of your real dad and afraid of losing your love. If talking to your mom doesn't help you understand what's really going on, try talking to a school counselor or another adult you trust.

My mom listens in on my phone calls!

She Hears Everything!

Dear Ali,

My mom always listens to my phone conversations on speakerphone downstairs while I am upstairs with the phone. I can't stand it! I have asked her to please stop and she just says, "Well, what are you talking about that you don't want me to hear?" Please help. It's embarrassing because my friend and boyfriend ask why she does it. I am almost 13!

–No Privacy

Dear No Privacy,

It sounds like your mom is having a little trouble getting used to your growing up! Maybe she feels listening in is the *only* way she'll find out what's going on in your life. This is probably the *last* thing you want to do now, but it may help if you make an extra effort to fill her in on what's happening with you and your friends. Remind her that wanting some privacy doesn't mean you're talking about anything bad or wrong, and that your friends feel uncomfortable knowing she's listening in. Present your case calmly. Getting angry will only increase the chances that your mom will think you want to keep your conversations private because you have something to hide.

ali

Sneaky Sister

Dear Ali,

My little sister is getting really mean. If I do one little thing to upset her, she hits me or calls me names. When I tell my parents, they don't believe me because they don't see it or hear it, and because she's littler than I am. What should I do?

—Can't Take It

Dear Can't Take It,

Unfortunately it's often true that the youngest child gets the benefit of the doubt when there's trouble between siblings. If your parents don't believe your side, you'll have to try to change her behavior on your own. The next time she's behaving badly, head for your room and close the door for a while. When you are both feeling calm again, tell your sister that you don't like being with her when she hits you and calls you names. Then praise her for the nice things she does, and tell her how much you like it when she acts that way. Keep your cool and use *compliments* as your defense. You may be able to change her behavior for the better.

ali

Mom Won't Budge

Dear Ali,

Every time I lift my arm up, my friends make fun of me because I have hair under my arms. I also have hair on my legs. I already asked my mom if I could shave but she said I was too young. None of my other friends have hair under their arms yet and they are all allowed to shave their legs. I need help, Ali!

—Feeling Hairy

Dear Feeling Hairy,

It's hard when you're developing faster than your friends. And it's worth trying to talk to your mom again. Approach her at a time when she can really listen to you, and be positive—no whining or begging! Tell her that not being allowed to shave makes you feel different from other girls your age and makes you self-conscious. If she still thinks you're too young to shave, ask her to help you shop for clothes that will allow you to feel more comfortable, like shirts with sleeves, and Capris instead of shorts. Your willingness to find another solution might help your mom see how much the situation disturbs you. If not, at least your friends won't have as much opportunity to tease you.

ali

Chapter Three

BOYS

YOUR TOP 3 BOY-RELATED PROBLEMS ARE:

- Not knowing if your crush likes you.
- Pressure to have a boyfriend.
- A boy likes you but you don't like him back.

DG POLL!

If you could ask a boy just one question, what would it be?

What's up with all the rough-housing?	12%
Do boys like it when girls ask them out?	18%
Nothing! Let them keep their old secrets.	20%
Why do some boys spread rumors about girls?	50%

Tell or Not?

Dear Ali,

I have the biggest crush on this boy, but he's one of my friends. He used to be my closest friend back in fourth grade, but then I moved to a new school. Now in seventh grade, we're best buds again. I want to tell him how I feel but I don't know how he feels about me, and I don't want to ruin our friendship. How can I let him know how I feel without endangering our friendship?

—So Confused

Dear So Confused,

This is tricky. Friendship can sometimes blossom into something more, but if you confess your feelings and he doesn't feel the same way, you may end up feeling so awkward around each other that it will be hard to stay friends. And even if he's also crushing on you and you start going out, how long is it likely to last? It will be hard to go back to being "just" friends. If you feel it's worth it to risk the friendship, go for it. But if you're not sure, it may be better to wait a while. If you're still crushing on him in a few months, you can always reconsider. But once you've let him know how you feel, you can't take it back.

ali

I have the biggest crush on this boy...

Angry BFF

Dear Ali,

I just got a boyfriend and my BFF now hates me and says I don't spend enough time with her! And worst of all, when he comes on the playground, my BFF says, "Here's your cue to ditch me and play with him!" What do I do?

—Stuck in the Middle

Dear Stuck in the Middle,

Sounds like a classic case of "boyfriend-itis"! If your BFF's observations are accurate, you're doing what lots of girls do: Ditching your old friends for a crush. She doesn't hate you— she's just sad, lonely, and jealous of your relationship with this boy. Try putting yourself in her place: Imagine that *she's* the one with the boyfriend, and all of a sudden she's with *him* when you wish she was with *you*. See? The trick to keeping your friendship strong is to talk it through and make compromises. Let her know that she's still your BFF and that her friendship is important to you. Find ways that the three of you can hang out together, and be sure to spend some time with just her.

ali

Like Me, Please!

Dear Ali,

I have a huge crush on this boy at my school. I've done everything in my power to impress him. I dress nicely and I changed my hairstyle. I even became a basketball fan because he loves basketball. But it's like he doesn't know I exist. He's in some of my classes and I want to talk to him but I always get too nervous. How can I get him to notice me?

—Invisible

Dear Invisible,

Your best bet for getting someone to notice you is to start up a relaxed, friendly conversation. And how about being *yourself*? Instead of dressing up for him, wear something you feel good wearing, and do your hair the way *you* like it. It will be easier to relax around him if you feel like yourself. And if you're faking an interest in basketball just to get his attention, it's bound to fail in the long run. So stop worrying so much about impressing him, and concentrate on just being yourself. Try saying hi in class and asking him what he thought of a homework assignment. You'll feel more comfortable around him, and talking to him will be much easier.

Still Hoping

Dear Ali,

I like this guy in my class, but he doesn't like me back. We were friends a few years ago and I thought he liked me but I guess I was wrong. My friends say things like, "Why do you like him? You know he doesn't like you!" I've liked him for the past four years but he <u>still</u> doesn't like me. Should I give up on love?

—Desperate

Dear Desperate,

You should *never* give up on love! But sometimes you *do* have to let go of a crush if it's not returned. It may be that your friends are tired of you crushing on a guy who just isn't going to respond. (They just want what's best for you!) It can be hard to let go and move on, but it sounds like that's what you need to do. Focus on other things in your life, and the people that *do* give you attention. Hang out with friends, and vow *not* to talk about boys. Read a lot. Do some extra credit projects. Before you know it, someone new might catch your eye—and this time maybe the feelings will be mutual!

ali

Dear Ali,

I have two friends who became boyfriend and girl-friend. At first it was great, but then he started to gang up on me with some other girls. He's always calling me names and making fun of me. I have learned to ignore them, but when he saw that it wasn't making me leave my friend (his girlfriend) he started to tell her lies about me. She and I have talked about it, but she says she has to see him <u>do</u> something in order to take sides. I need some help!

—BFF's BF Problem

Dear BFF's BF Problem,

Whoa! Several things are happening here. First, I'd bet that the boyfriend is jealous of your friendship with his girlfriend. It sounds like he wants her to just focus on *him* and not on her girlfriends. And if your girlfriend doesn't believe you when you tell her what's going on, maybe she's not as close a friend as you thought. It might be a good idea to spend time with other friends until she gets her priorities straightened out. Sometimes we do lose sight of friendships when we're interested in a boy—but in the end, it's those friendships that matter the most! Hopefully, she'll get it sorted out and realize that she needs to show you a little more loyalty.

My friends want me to have a boyfriend...

Dear Ali,

My friends have boyfriends and we're only 10! They keep trying to get me to hook up with this guy I really like, but I'm not ready to have a boyfriend. Every time we have a fight, they say I'm jealous because they have boyfriends, but I'm not jealous. I would really like to have a boyfriend at some point, but I'm not ready. Should I go ahead and have a boyfriend, or should I wait?

—Being Pushed

Dear Being Pushed,

Some girls like a special boy when they're eight and some girls don't find someone they care about until college. There are no rules about when to have a boyfriend, so you need to do what feels right for you. Don't make a big deal out of it when your friends suggest that you hook up with your crush. Just say something like, "Thanks for trying to help, but I'm just not interested." When they claim that you're jealous, say something similar. The trick is not to get worked up. If your friends just can't understand, you might want to start developing some new friendships with girls who aren't so focused on boyfriends.

ali

Same Guy!

Dear Ali,

I used to have a crush on the same guy as my best friend, but I never told her because she might get mad. Then a couple of weeks ago she started going out with him. I try not to like him so much but I can't help it. I'm really jealous, and I don't want to be around her when she's talking about him (like, all the time). I think she knows something's wrong, but I can't tell her what it is. How can I stop liking him? Help!

-Crushed

Dear Crushed,

Unfortunately, you can't make yourself feel (or not feel) something. Try not to hang out with your BFF and her boyfriend any more than you have to. Keep busy with other activities and put some effort into making friends with other guys. You should also talk to your friend, even if it's scary. She already knows something is wrong, so she's probably imagining it's something even worse. Be sure to tell her how important she is to you and ask her not to talk about him too much around you, or ask you to hang out with the two of them. Then give her some time to get used to the idea. And with time, your feelings for him will fade.

ali

Dear Ali,

I have a crush on a boy in my class. The problem is that he is my best guy friend. The problem is also that I <u>used</u> to like him and then I stopped, and I told him that I don't like him anymore—but now I like him <u>again</u>! Should I tell him?

—On Again, Off Again

Dear On Again, Off Again,

Hmmm...are you confused? Chances are this boy is! Sounds like you've got a good friendship going, so before you complicate matters by telling him you've changed your mind again, stop and think. Why did you stop liking him? Why did you start again? Is this really about your feelings for him, or are you just enjoying the drama? (Be honest!) If you sincerely like him and are willing to risk your friendship to go out with him, tell him how you feel. Otherwise, it might be wiser to keep your lips zipped.

About to Quit

Dear Ali,

I'm the only girl on my soccer team, but I'm not that great. The boys are always telling me how bad I am, and it really upsets me. I'm even thinking about quitting, but I really want to play. What should I do?

—Soccer Sad

Dear Soccer Sad,

You're a true sport for hanging in there in the face of those critical boys! The most important thing is that you *keep playing*! You can't control how they treat you, but you *can* work on not letting their words upset you. More to the point, you can work on your soccer skills and, yes, improve! If you practice hard and keep playing, you *will* get better. And when the boys realize you're serious, they'll tease you less and give you the respect you deserve. Just don't let them chase you away from doing something you love. Instead, look at this as a challenge and keep on kicking. And good luck!

ali

Dear Ali,

There is this boy who has been my friend. Then one day he told me that he likes me! I never had feelings for him before, but now I think I like him. Are these feelings real or what? I don't want to think I like him if it's only because he said he likes me. What should I do?

—Unsure

Dear Unsure,

Confusing stuff, huh? Maybe you *do* like this boy, but it took hearing that he has a crush on you to make you think that. It's also possible that you just like the *idea* of having a boyfriend, and you've convinced yourself you like him because you know he likes you. Ultimately, you're the only one who can decide what's going on. Sit yourself down and ask yourself these questions:

- If you stay "just friends" and he gets a girlfriend, will you be jealous?
- Do you want a boyfriend just because it seems like everyone else does?
- Do you think having a boyfriend would make you more popular—and is that important to you?

Be honest with yourself! You'll figure out what you truly want.

He likes me... I don't like him.

So Not Crushed

Dear Ali,

This guy in my class likes me, but I don't like him. He's telling all his friends that I like him. He wrote a note to me asking me to be his girlfriend. I just want to work on schoolwork and not worry about having a boyfriend. Anyway, I'm too young to be thinking about that. How do I make him stop? I've tried everything.

—No Boyfriend for Me

Dear No Boyfriend for Me,

You can't make this boy stop liking you, but hopefully your actions can make him keep his feelings to himself. Even if you've talked to him already, try doing so one more time. Don't make a big deal of it—just find a minute and say something like, "I'm sorry, but I don't want a boyfriend right now. I just don't like you like that." If it's too hard to tell him face-to-face, write a very brief note. And let that be the end of it as far as you're concerned. Make sure your friends know where you stand. Then it won't matter what he says. He might keep on sending you notes and gossiping, but if you don't respond, he'll probably stop.

I Want Out!

Dear Ali,

All my friends ever talk about is their boyfriends and I got tired of always being left out. So when this boy in my class asked me out I said yes. It was okay at first but I'm getting really sick of it now. He always wants to hang out at school, and he texts me at night and he even brings me presents sometimes. I don't want to hurt his feelings but I don't want a boyfriend anymore. What do I do?

—Tired of BF

Dear Tired of BF,

You need to tell him. His feelings might be a little hurt at first, but it's better to tell him the truth than to let him go on thinking you like him as much as he likes you. (And it sounds like he really does like you!) Just tell him nicely that you enjoy being friends with him but you've realized that you're just not ready to have a boyfriend yet. And the next time a boy asks you out, think about how you really feel before saying yes. If you like the *idea* of having a boyfriend more than you like the boy, tell him you're not interested.

ali

Does He Like Me?

Dear Ali,

I have a huge crush on this boy at my school. He's really, really cute, and he always cracks jokes and makes me laugh. I really want to know if he likes me back but I'm afraid to ask him. How can I tell?

−Totally Crushed

Dear Totally Crushed,

If he cracks jokes when you're around he's probably trying to get your attention and likes making you laugh. Sometimes boys do drop hints like that. He might also try to find excuses to be near you or to talk to you, like passing your desk on the way to the pencil sharpener four times a day, or texting you every night for the math assignment. He might also tease you more than he teases other girls, although hopefully not in a mean way. On the other hand, some boys are too shy to drop hints, so it's entirely possible that he likes you even if he *doesn't* do these things. (Confusing, huh?) Sometimes you just might have to wonder...and hope.

ali

Chapter Four

SCHOOL

WHEN IT COMES TO SCHOOL, YOU WORRY MOST ABOUT:

- Fitting in.
- Balancing your many activities.
- Getting bullied.

DG POLL!

What's your favorite part of the school day?

Being in class—I like to learn!	11%
P.E. It's hard to sit in a desk all day!	13%
Hearing the final bell.	24%
Hanging out with my friends at lunch and recess.	52%

Anything for Friendship?

Dear Ali,

There is a girl in my class that I really want to be friends with. She is more popular than me at school but we go to the same church and sometimes we hang out there. Sometimes she is nice to me at church but most of the time she ignores me at school. Last week we were taking a Spanish test and she started looking at my answers. I told her not to, but she made this sad face so I let her. Afterwards she said I could sit with her and her friends at lunch. I want to be her friend but I don't want to be a cheater. What should I do?

—Not a Cheater

Dear Not a Cheater,

You're right not to want to be a cheater, so don't let this girl turn you into one! If she's only nice to you when she wants something from you, she's using you. You may enjoy being a little more popular for a little while after you help her out, but is that really worth losing your self-respect? Stay true to what you know is right, and stick to real friends who like you for who you are, not what you can do for them. You deserve no less.

ali

I want to be friends, but I don't want to cheat!

Want to Improve

Dear Ali,

I used to be a straight-A student. Now I feel my grades are dropping, but only in math. I'm great in every other subject. But I still want to do better. My friends look up to me and I usually help them when they need help on something, but now I can't. I'm scared to even show them my grades. I guess I just don't understand math anymore. How can I do better?

-Math Frazzled

Dear Math Frazzled,

It sounds like you're a great student! If you've been used to getting good grades without much effort, it can be frustrating the first time you really have to work for a grade, but that doesn't mean it's time to give up. Try talking to your teacher. Explain that you want to do your best, and ask her how you can get some extra help. Maybe ask if there's some extra-credit you can do. In the meantime keep on working with your friends. They won't think less of you for having to work harder, and you may even be able to help each other. So figure out what's wrong, work to change it, and don't give up on yourself so easily!

ali

New Start, New Fears

Dear Ali,

I have a problem. I am going to a new middle school in September and I am scared that I will not be able to get to the right classes on time and that I will be late for every class. The other problem is that I am going from a tiny grade school to a really big middle school and high school. What if I get lost or can't find my locker?

—Scared Student

Dear Scared Student,

A lot of kids feel this way when they're starting a new, bigger school, so you're not alone. Many schools have an orientation day for the new class coming in to make that first day less scary. They'll probably give you a map and help you find your locker and your classrooms. If your school doesn't have an orientation day or you just want to be extra-sure you'll know your way around, ask your parents to call the school and arrange to visit during summer break. Also, don't stress out thinking you'll be late and get in trouble. As long as you're careful not to stop and chat between classes, you should have enough time to get where you're going.

War of the Words

Dear Ali,

A lot of people in my school call me really bad names. I try to ignore them, but I just can't because it hurts my feelings. I need some advice!

—Hurting

Dear Hurting,

Words can hurt, and it's hard to ignore them, as you've found out! It might help to think of the comments as rain that just washes over you and drains away—it can't hurt you or stay with you. Another approach is to surprise the name-callers with an unexpected response like, "I like being me just fine, thanks," or "Have a nice day!" In the meantime, remember what a terrific girl you are, and that they are the ones with the real problem, not you! And if all else fails, find a moment to talk to your teacher when other kids aren't around—she should be able to help.

ali

Dear Ali,

I have a huge problem focusing on schoolwork. When I'm at school it's a little easier because there aren't as many distractions, but at home it's a disaster. My brothers call me a procrastinator and I'm starting to agree with them. I can't focus. A few years ago the doctor said I probably have ADD, but the next year my teacher said I am "too smart" to have it. How can I concentrate? Can you help me?

—Procrastinator

Dear Procrastinator,

First, don't label yourself a procrastinator! Now, do you have an area that's just for homework—a table or desk that's quiet, well-lit, and away from any distractions like people, music, or television? Then, when it's time to do math, take out only the things you need for math. When that's done, put everything away and take out only what you need for the next subject. As you complete each assignment, give yourself a little reward: Listen to one song on your iPod or read five pages of a fun book. If you really try but still don't see an improvement, ask your parents for help. It may be time to consult your doctor again, or find a tutor to help you study.

ali

I need help in math...

Dear Ali,

My grades in math are really low because I didn't get math during sixth grade. But in a few months I'm going to seventh grade. How am I going to understand that kind of math without knowing the other? I also asked for tutoring programs after school, but I <u>still</u> don't get it. All the other kids, even my friends, get it but I don't, and my teacher is a little harsh sometimes.

— Math Dummy

Dear Math Dummy,

You're no dummy. It's very smart of you to ask for help at the tutoring program and to recognize that you need more help to succeed next year. Tell your parents that you're frustrated but that you don't want to give up. Ask them if you can work with a private tutor over the summer. If that's not possible, talk to your seventh grade math teacher on the first day of school and let her know that you want extra help to catch up. You might even ask your friends for help, too. Everyone's brain works differently, and you probably just need to find someone who can explain the concepts in a way that makes sense to you. If you keep trying, you'll get there.

So Little Time

Dear Ali,

I love to be involved at school. I'm on the yearbook staff, student council, in a book club, and I have a couple of other activities, too, plus one thing at church. I also want to join a school sports team and start guitar lessons, but if I were in sports I would have to give up a lot of other activities. And my mom says I can't take guitar lessons because I've got too much on my plate, but I think I could take it once a week. What should I do?

—Overwhelmed

Dear Overwhelmed,

Wow! It's amazing that you're so involved! Try making a list of everything, including the activities you'd *like* to be doing. Put them in order of how important they are to you. Then add a note next to each about how much time and/or money it takes, and when you'll need rides. Having it all written down will help you see how much of a time commitment you and your mom are making, as well as how balanced your activities are. Try to come to an agreement with your mom on which activities are best for you. (Be prepared to fight for your top choices!) This will show your mom that you've thought this through and understand the commitments you're both making.

Dear Ali,

The kids at my school like me because of my things, not because of who I am. Even though I show them what a good person I am, they don't care! What should I do?

-Liked for the Wrong Reasons

Dear Liked for the Wrong Reasons,

Wow—you're asking an important and tough question! It sounds like you may need to place less importance on your possessions for a while in order to strike a better balance with your friends. Try inviting them to do something other than come to your house and play with your stuff. Arrange to meet at the park, or go to the mall or the movies. Spending more time away from all your things will help you to feel more comfortable and give your friends a chance to get to know the real you better.

Dear Ali,

There's a girl at school who's always mean to me. She calls me names, bugs me, and yells at me! I want her to leave me alone. I'm scared to compete against her, because I'm worried I'll lose and she'll make fun of me. I've already told the teacher and tried ignoring her, and I even tried talking it out with her, but nothing seems to stop her. It's getting so I don't want to go to school anymore. What should I do?

—Tried Everything

Dear Tried Everything,

This girl is definitely the one with the problem—but unfortunately, she's taking it out on you! You've already tried lots of great options to work this out. If talking to your teacher hasn't helped, it's time to get your parents involved. Ask if the three of you can have a conference with your teacher. The harassment should not be allowed to continue. If your school has a "peer mediation" group, you might ask to try this option also. In that case, you and the girl would talk with the help of someone your own age who does not take sides and who helps each of you to see the other's point of view.

Too Smart?

Dear Ali,

I'm really smart in school. My teacher makes up review games for tests, and when I go against someone, they always say, "Oh, I'm gonna lose. I better just not play." It hurts my feelings. One day, I even <u>let</u> someone win because they said that. I like being smart because of good grades, but I don't want to be picked on. (I do have friends, and my best friend always sticks up for me) What should I do? Get over it and hang out with my real friends, or act stupid for the rest of my life?

—Miss Einstein

Dear Miss Einstein,

This seems like an easy choice: Hang out with your real friends and show your smarts! It's much better to develop a thicker skin than to hide your brains. Here's something else you might try: The next time someone says there's no point in playing against you, compliment her. "Math does come easy to me, but I can't run as fast as you." Show her you're not that concerned about who wins by saying, "I just want to get ready for the test." Being generous toward the other person may help her feel less insecure. And if all else fails, think about this: If you're going to be teased about something, isn't it better that it's for a positive quality, like being smart?

Dear Ali,

I have a lot going on, and I keep forgetting about my homework. I'm really busy taking care of my family's new puppy, doing chores, and being involved with my friends. Plus my parents keep telling me to clean my room. I try to be neat but then my room gets messy again. It's the same drill every day. At the end of the day I'm so tired that I forget about my homework. Help me, please.

—Too Busy

Dear Too Busy,

Sounds like it's time to reorder your priorities! If you leave your homework until the very end of the day, you're bound to be too tired to do it well—or even to do it at all. It *is* important to get your chores done, and that puppy is counting on you for good care, but your schoolwork really should come before being involved with your friends. Try getting your homework and chores done as soon as you get home from school. Write up a schedule of your assignments and chores, and as you finish each item on it, check it off. After everything is done, you can relax and hang out with your friends.

Chapter Five

GROWING UP

GROWING UP IS TOUGH! YOU'RE WORRIED THAT:

- You're the first—or the last—to develop.
- You need to lose weight.
- You can't keep up with all the responsibilities.

DG POLL!

What scares you most about growing up?

Nothing—I'm ready!	16%
Even more responsibilities.	16%
Drifting away from friends.	22%
Puberty!	46%

Changing Too Fast

Dear Ali,

We just watched the sex education tape in school. I'm the only girl in my class with a chest. So when it came to the part about breasts and bras, all the girls started looking and even pointing at me. Now I feel really awkward around everyone, even my best friends. I'm not sure how to react or what to say. Please help me!

— Awkward Outcast

Dear Awkward Outcast,

You don't have to say anything, actually. Just ignore the girls who aren't your friends; they're probably just curious— or envious!—and didn't mean to hurt your feelings or make you feel self-conscious. You don't have to say anything to your best friends, either, if you prefer not to. But if you trust them not to tease you, you might feel better if you clear the air. Tell them you feel a little awkward being the first to develop. They will all be going through the same thing soon enough, and it will help all of you if you can talk about it. Isn't that what are friends for?

ali

I'm the only girl in my class with a chest.

Right or Wrong?

Dear Ali,

My friend Anaya is very chubby, and everyone is always making fun of her just because she is overweight. We work out and she lost 35 pounds but everyone still makes fun of me for hanging out with her. I'm starting to think there's something wrong with me. Am I doing the right thing? I need advice.

—Teased Friend

Dear Teased Friend,

There's nothing wrong with you—in fact, you're a great friend! It's always the right thing to stand by your friends when others are teasing. And not only are you standing by Anaya, you're helping her to get healthier by working out together! If someone makes fun of you for hanging out with her, either ignore them completely, or say something like, "She's a good friend." Either way, keep your response brief and matter-of-fact. If they see they can't get you upset, the teasers will stop.

ali

Dear Ali,

I'm going through puberty and my mood changes a lot. For example, I was playing with my friend and I was all happy and everything. Then, all of a sudden, I got really mean and he said, "If you don't stop being mean, I'll just go home!" I didn't know what to do! What can I do about it?

—Moody Girl

Dear Moody Girl,

Moodiness *is* a part of puberty. Your body is producing all kinds of new hormones and they can put you on an emotional roller coaster. You can't do much about that, but you can be extra careful about how you act. If you feel a bad mood coming on, try retreating to your room for a while. It will also help to have an outlet for your feelings, like writing poems, drawing, or playing or listening to music. If a bad mood gets the best of you and you say something you regret, apologize immediately and explain that you didn't mean it. Hang in there—your hormone levels will even out, and you'll be able to get off that roller coaster and feel normal again.

ali

Overweight and Okay?

Dear Ali,

I'm fat. It seems weird for me to be saying this. I don't know if people talk about how fat I am behind my back, but I don't care. At least I used to not care. I used to think, "This is who I am," and "People have to accept me for the way I am, and if they don't, that's up to them." Should I still follow the rule that "If my friends try to change me then they aren't really my friends?" Can you help me? I weigh 220 pounds and I'm 11.

–Fat

Dear Fat,

Do you feel like your friends are trying to change you because they're concerned about your well-being and happiness? If so, mentioning your weight does not necessarily mean that they are not good friends. What's important is why they've brought it up. They may sincerely want you to be healthier, to be active in sports, and to be able to wear cute clothes. They may even be concerned that your feelings could be hurt by other kids teasing you about your weight. If that's so, they have your best interests at heart and are still your friends. But if they mention your weight in a mean way and seem to want to hurt your feelings or put you down, they're not acting like true friends.

ali

Stop Being Me?

Dear Ali,

I've been playing soccer for four years, and I love it. But this year I joined a new team, and I'm nothing like the other girls! I'm not skinny, and when I miss a shot, they all yell at me! My mom keeps telling me, "Be yourself." Well, I've been myself my _entire_ _life_ and it's still not working. I feel like a loser. Can you help?

—Soccer Loser

Dear Soccer Loser,

Hey—you're not a _loser_! You sound like a girl with a great sense of who you are, and your mom is right: You _should_ go on being your amazing self. So what else can you do? You and your mom might try having a talk with the coach. Explain that you're uncomfortable with all the negative comments when you miss a shot. Ask the coach to talk to the team, not about you specifically, but about how teammates should treat each other. Keep projecting a positive self-image and doing what you love (playing soccer), and the other girls will accept you for who you are, even if you're not just like them.

Dear Ali,

All of my brothers and sisters say that I'm fat, but my mom does not. But sometimes I think that she's lying to me. I think maybe I am fat, but I don't know who to believe.

−Am I Fat?

Dear Am I Fat?,

Sometimes brothers and sisters say thoughtless things. You need to sit down with your mom and discuss the situation. Tell her that you honestly want to know if you are too heavy to be healthy. If talking to your mom doesn't reassure you, ask her if she can make an appointment with your doctor, who can tell you if your weight is in the normal, healthy range for your age and height. If you need to lose weight, your doctor can help you. But if it turns out that your brothers and sisters are just being mean, tune them out. What matters is what you know to be true.

ali

Life Is Unfair

Dear Ali,

I don't feel good about myself. When I look in a mirror, I feel like breaking it. I think the reason I don't have friends is because I'm ugly. I even have a paper in my pocket that says, "I hate myself!" I want to feel good about myself, but I feel miserable. I even cry about this! Please, Ali, help me!

—Hating Myself

Dear Hating Myself,

The first thing you need to do is tear that piece of paper up and throw it away. Then write a new note that says, "I love myself." Put that in your pocket instead. You also need to talk to an adult about how you feel. We all have moments when we feel down, but you shouldn't go through life hating yourself. If you can't talk to your mom or dad, is there another adult, like a teacher, who listens to you and that you trust? If the first person you talk to doesn't help you, try someone else. Keep asking for help, because there is help out there. You deserve to feel good about yourself—and if you keep trying, you will.

ali

Don't Want to Grow Up

Dear Ali,

I never want to grow up. I just want to stay the same forever. My friends think I'm really weird since I read comics and watch cartoons like a little kid, and even my mom says I <u>have</u> to grow up. Every time I'm with my friends, I have to hide my real hobbies and what I like. It doesn't interfere with my education, so I can't see why I should start growing up, just because my friends and family want me to.

            —Forever Young

Dear Forever Young,

Everyone "grows up" at different times and in different ways. There are adults who never really "grow up" in the way some people might think they should, and kids who grow up much too fast in some ways. Whether we like it or not, things *do* change—no one can stop time from passing. But that doesn't mean you have to give up your interests. In fact, it's really cool that you've stuck with what you like, in spite of the pressure to change. Maybe you could try doing some babysitting—that way you'd be doing a "grown up" thing, but you would also be playing with younger kids who have the same interests as you.

A "Big" Problem

Dear Ali,

My friend Kaitlyn and I are taller than most kids in our grade. We're also the only two girls in our grade who are more developed physically. I often look at my other friends and think how incredibly petite and skinny they are. And sometimes popular girls and guys tease me, saying things like, "You're gross! You have big jugs!" or snapping my bra strap constantly to embarrass me. One even grabbed a pad from my backpack and laughed. And they only do it to me, not Kaitlyn! I'm getting tired of it! Please help!

—Annoyed at My Body

Dear Annoyed at My Body,

It's always tough to be the first girl in a group to hit puberty. Kids tease because they want attention, they're jealous, or they think putting someone else down makes them cool. In other words, their teasing has more to do with them than anything to do with you. Still, it might help to look at how you're reacting to them. They may go after you because they think it's fun to watch you react. Instead of getting angry or embarrassed, act like it's no big deal. Or try a little humor. When someone comments about your size, say something like, "Really? Wow—I hadn't noticed." It won't be easy, but you'll get your final revenge one day. Everyone else *will* catch up!

ali

I'm tired of being picked on...

Feeling Different

Dear Ali,

I used to wear leg braces because of the way I walked. If I didn't wear them, I would have had to get an operation. Now I have to wear them again. My friends and other people in my grade always ask me questions about them. It really hurts my feelings and I get embarrassed. I want to be treated just like everyone else because I have been called names my whole life. Help!

−Braced

Dear Braced,

It's terrible that you've been called names your whole life—that stinks! But like it or not, people are going to be curious about your leg braces, and their questions aren't necessarily an attempt to be mean. If they're just curious, you might say, "I have a problem with my legs and these braces are helping to correct it." You don't have to tell them any more if you don't want to. If they keep asking questions, tell them you appreciate their interest but you'd rather talk about something else. As for the teasers, I know it's not easy, but ignore them. The more you show that you accept your leg braces and aren't bothered by them, the more other people will accept them, too.

Not Good Enough?

Dear Ali,

I'm in the advanced math class at my school, and there's this girl in my class who is so much smarter than I am. She's always first to finish math problems, she always aces tests, and she always does extra credit on her homework. Aside from all of that, she is a junior professional dancer. She's been in "The Nutcracker" about a million times. It makes me feel so dumb and untalented. Is she wicked smart or am I just really dumb?

—Feeling Dumb

Dear Feeling Dumb,

It sounds like this girl *is* smart and talented...and it also sounds like you're jealous. That's a natural emotion, and you're not the first girl who has ever felt it—we all have. But here's the thing about life: You can *always* find someone smarter, prettier, or more talented than you are, but why look at the world like that? Her many gifts don't detract from your own talents and abilities (and you *do* have them). And if you want to get better grades in math or learn how to dance, figure out what you need to do to reach those goals. But do it because you want to be the best *you* can be, not because you're jealous of her.

ali

Chapter Six

TOUGH STUFF

YOUR TOUGHEST "TOP 3":

- Your parents' divorce.
- Having someone you love die.
- Keeping a really big secret.

DG POLL!

What helps you get through a tough time?

Hugging my old teddy bear.	9%
Hanging out with my pet.	10%
Talking with my parents.	10%
Leaning on my friends.	24%
All of the above!	47%

I don't want to choose...

Can't Choose!

Dear Ali,

My parents are divorced. I have a stepmom now and she really loves me, but my mom doesn't want me to accept her. I love my stepmom, and when I'm 12, I'll have to choose between my mom, or my dad and stepmom. What should I do? I only have two years to decide. Please help me, Ali.

-Two Moms

Dear Two Moms,

I'd bet your mom is scared of losing you! Maybe she thinks that if she keeps you from accepting your stepmom now, you won't leave her later on. You need to talk to her. Tell her that you love her and that you will always be her daughter, but that you love and need your dad, too. Remind her that although you care about your stepmom, she could never take your mom's place and that your stepmom isn't a threat to her, but something good for you. (How could you have too many people to love you?) And don't worry too much about having to make the decision now. You'll be much more ready to decide when the time comes.

ali

Problem Dad

Dear Ali,

My dad is an alcoholic, and he travels a lot for his work. My mom says that they can never live together because my dad can only stay sober for about a week. He barely comes home, and most of his money goes to alcohol. I miss him a lot and I don't know what to do. Everyone is always talking about how much fun they have when they spend time with their dads, but I can't. And my dad always calls when he's drunk and makes me cry, and then my mom and dad get in a fight. What should I do?

-Drunk Dad

Dear Drunk Dad,

Alcoholism is a difficult disease to deal with, and no one can really help your dad until he decides he's ready. Until then, your mom is doing the right thing by not letting him live with you. You also shouldn't have to talk to him when he's drunk. It will be difficult, but tell him, "Dad, I love you, but I don't want to talk to you when you've been drinking. It upsets me too much." Hopefully your dad will be ready to get help soon, for both your sakes. Until then, ask your mom to look into Alateen, a program for kids with alcoholic parents. Alateen can help you understand his problem better, and teach you the best ways to deal with it.

ali

Family Falling Apart

Dear Ali,

I feel so lonely. My dad passed away last year, and now my mom is always partying, going on dates, or on the computer. She never pays any attention to me. My brothers don't like me, either—they wish I were somewhere else. I don't have any friends. I used to think some of the girls in a grade above me were my friends, but lately they seem to be avoiding me. I don't have anybody to talk to, share my feelings with, or hang out with. I need some advice.

—Totally Lost

Dear Totally Lost,

I'm so sorry—it's really hard to lose someone so important to you. But it sounds like you're clear about what you're feeling and what you need, and that's a good first step to getting some help. Try writing a letter to your mom explaining that you wish you could spend more time together. It would also be a good idea to talk about your feelings to your school counselor. As for friends, invite over a girl in your own grade. It may take some time, but if you remember to stay open and positive, you will find a friend your own age to trust and confide in. And although you will always miss him, your sadness about your dad will become easier to bear with time.

Out-of-Control Friend

Dear Ali,

I have a friend who is my age (11), and she is going out with her next-door-neighbor, who is 17. She isn't even supposed to be going out! She threatens everybody if they try to tell. She said the 17-year-old has already kissed her! He takes her shopping and everything. I have no clue what to do! Please, Ali, help me!

—Unsure

☆ ☆ ☆

Dear Unsure,

It's understandable that you don't want to tell on your friend, but it sounds like you have good reason to be worried about her. An 11-year-old should not be dating a 17-year-old! So—in spite of the girl's threats—this is one of those times when it's okay to betray a confidence. Tell your parents or an adult you trust what's going on. Yes, it may cost you the girl's friendship, at least for a while. But think about it: If a friend is truly headed for trouble, isn't letting an adult know the right thing to do?

Dear Ali,

Lately I've been worrying a lot. I'm afraid terrorists are going to bomb my house or blow up my neighborhood. Or maybe there will be a hurricane and my house will get destroyed. Then I can't get to sleep. My mom says to just not think about it, but I don't know how to stop.

—Can't Sleep

Dear Can't Sleep,

You're not alone—a lot of people are worried these days. It's hard to deal with fears about things we can't control, and nighttime always seems to make everything scarier. The best thing you can do is to talk about your fears during the daytime when they're less overwhelming. Remind yourself that no matter how terrible the evening news is, we live in a very safe country. There's no guarantee that everything in your life will be okay, but the chance of anything bad happening to you because of terrorists or hurricanes is very, very small. Finally, avoid watching the news or scary shows at night. Instead, try watching a show or reading a book that makes you laugh. You'll get to sleep more easily.

ali

My best friend has cancer, and I want to help.

Ask Ali: All The Advice You'll Ever Need

Dear Ali,

I just found out that my best friend has cancer. I want to talk to her about it but I don't know what to say. I feel so nervous whenever I am around her. I am afraid I will say the wrong thing and make her feel worse. I am so sad and I want to help her so badly but I don't know what to do.

—Want to Help

Dear Want to Help,

Your friend is lucky to have a friend who cares so much about her. The best thing you can do is to tell her how you feel. Explain that you care about her and that you want to help, but that you're afraid of saying or doing the wrong thing. Ask her what she'd like you to do, and then honor her wishes. If she wants to talk about what she's going through, be there to listen. If she doesn't, find fun things to do to distract her from her troubles. Whatever you do, stick by her—the *last* thing she needs is to lose her best friend on top of everything she's going through. You'll *both* feel better if you keep talking.

Dad Doesn't Understand

Dear Ali,

I suffer from anxiety and when I have to leave the house I start to get sick. We got a therapist to help my anxiety go away. My parents are divorced and my dad dislikes my therapist. My dad makes me mad a lot, but the most recent thing was when he said that I was worthless if I didn't try to get over my anxiety. He is a nice guy but he really hurts me inside. The only people that I feel good talking to about all of this are my mom, my therapist, and my two best friends. How do I tell my dad how I feel? I don't want to hurt his feelings.

—Not Worthless

Dear Not Worthless,

Your dad may be a nice guy sometimes, but it's not very nice of him to tell you you're worthless, no matter what he thinks of your therapist or your anxiety problem. He *should* know how his comments make you feel, even if it does hurt his feelings. Have you talked to your therapist about telling him? Since she knows all about your relationship with your dad, she's probably the best person to help you figure out exactly what to say. You might also want to talk to your mom and your therapist about taking a break from visits with your dad for a while. You need to be surrounded by loving, supportive people while you're working through your anxiety.

ali

My stepdad is in jail.

Dad Doesn't Care?

Dear Ali,

My mom died a year ago and my dad does not care about her anymore. He's dating a teacher that I kind of like, but sometimes they have parties and show off, and I hate that! What should I do?

—Sad for My Mom

☆ ☆ ☆

Dear Sad for My Mom,

I'm so sorry that your mom died. That's something you will always be sad about, and I'm sure your dad will, too. And yet, as hard as it is to do, you both need to move on with your lives. I doubt your dad has really stopped caring about your mom. Instead, he may have decided that he needs to make a happy new life for *both* of you. It will help to talk to your dad about how you feel. He may not realize how upset you are, and he can probably reassure you that your mom is still very much in his heart—as she will always be in yours.

ali

Dear Ali,

I don't know what to do. I think my friend's dad is hurting her. One time she called and she was crying. She said, "He hit me again," but then the next day she said she didn't mean it and that she was just mad. But she sounded really upset and like she meant it, and she even had bruises on her arm. And she had more bruises yesterday. If I tell, she will get mad at me, but I don't want her to get hurt.

—Scared Friend

Dear Scared Friend,

You're a good friend for being so concerned. This is one of those situations where you *must* tell an adult. It's hard to know exactly what's going on with your friend, and it's really not something you can figure out on your own. Talk to your parents and let them know how worried you are. You should also tell a teacher, your school counselor, or the principal. If there are signs that your friend is being abused, they will help her. Your friend may be upset if she finds out that you told someone, but you will know you did the right thing by helping to keep her safe.

Why Are
Friendships So Confusing?

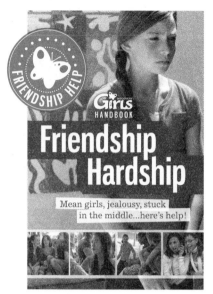

She knows everything about you...she'd never tell your secrets...she's your biggest fan. Who doesn't want a friend like that?

True friendship is a gift... but it can be hard to find. Whether you're stuck in a fading friendship, caught in the popularity trap, or dealing with mean girls, we'll break down the solutions to your problems step by step. Best of all, we'll teach you how to free yourself from poisonous friendships forever and be the best friend you can be.

Soon, you'll be meeting new people and making friends who truly respect and understand you...because you deserve first-rate friendships.

Look for this and other bestselling titles at DiscoveryGirls.com
ISBN 978-1-934766-09-5
$9.95

Getting Unstuck

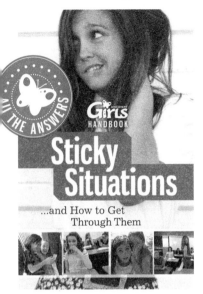

Remember when you got up the courage to tell your crush you liked him...and found out he didn't like you back? Didn't you wish you knew someone who had all the answers?

Well, have no fear! Not only do we know exactly how to handle your crush (what is wrong with him, anyway?), but we also know how to deal with a gazillion other sticky situations. Like when your BFF blabs your deepest secret to the entire school...or when you make a total fool of yourself onstage.

We'll also tell you how to handle being bullied by mean girls... or stranded at the mall...and much, much more! By the last page, you'll be ready to deal with anything!

Look for this and other bestselling titles at DiscoveryGirls.com
ISBN 978-1-934766-05-7
$9.95

Getting Over Bad Days

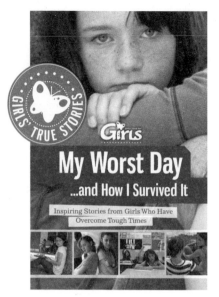

AUBRIE'S BEST FRIEND told her they couldn't be friends anymore because Aubrie was "too weird" to be seen with. Torrie was so upset when her parents divorced, she gained 20 pounds and let her grades go into freefall. Mackenzie watched her mom grow sicker and sicker and then die, just when Mackenzie needed her most.

In these amazing true stories, girls just like you share their private struggles, hoping to help you through your most difficult times.

You'll find comfort, encouragement, and inspiration here...and best of all, you'll know that whatever life throws at you, you are never alone.

Look for this and other bestselling titles at DiscoveryGirls.com
ISBN 978-1-934766-07-1
$9.95

INFORMATIVE, INSPIRING, HELPFUL AND FUN!

SUBSCRIBE TODAY!
$19.95/year
DiscoveryGirls.com

Discovery Girls is the magazine that gives girls ages 8 and up the advice, encouragement, and inspiration they need to get through the difficult tween years.

Created by girls, for girls, it's a forum for girls to help each other with tough issues like not fitting in, being caught in the middle, and the pressure to be perfect.

Plus, each is issue is packed with fun—quizzes, contests, embarrassing moments, fashion, and lots more!